LIFE ON A CHICKEN FARM

LIFE ON A
CHICKEN
FARM

by Judy Wolfman
photographs by David Lorenz Winston

Carolrhoda Books, Inc. / Minneapolis

We dedicate this book to the entire Martin family—Aaron, Emma Ruth, Loren, Jolene, Rosalyn, Jadon, and Ethan. Our thanks and appreciation for the many hours they spent helping us develop this book.

Also to the family of John H. Schwartz, Lancaster County Extension Director: We're thankful for the expert knowledge and advice John provided us about chickens. His contribution was invaluable.

—J.W. and D.L.W.

Carolrhoda Books, Inc.
A division of Lerner Publishing Group
241 First Avenue North
Minneapolis, MN 55401 U.S.A.

Website address: www.lernerbooks.com

Library of Congress Cataloging-in-Publication Data

Wolfman, Judy.
    Life on a chicken farm / by Judy Wolfman ; photographs by David Lorenz
Winston.
        p.   cm. — (Life on a farm)
    Summary: A child explains the activities taking place at home on a working
chicken farm.
    ISBN: 1–57505–191–5 (lib. bdg. : alk. paper)
    1. Chickens—Juvenile literature. 2. Farm life—Juvenile literature.
[1. Chickens. 2. Farm life.] I. Title: Chicken farm. II. Winston, David Lorenz,
ill. III. Title.
SF487.5.W66 2004
636.5'13—dc21   2002152919

Manufactured in the United States of America
1 2 3 4 5 6 – DP – 09 08 07 06 05 04

CONTENTS

CHICKENS
for Neighbors

I'm proud to work on my family's chicken farm.

How would you like to live next door to chickens? I live next to 95,000 of them, and I love it! My name is Loren Martin, and I live on a chicken farm with my family. Besides Mom and Dad, I have two sisters, Rosalyn and Jolene, and two brothers, Jadon and Ethan. We like working on the farm, because we do it as a family. And we like chickens, because they are fluffy and fun to take care of!

Our farm is called the Under His Wings Farm. We raise only chickens, not geese, ducks, or turkeys, like some **poultry** farmers do. And we raise our chickens for meat, not for eggs.

6

Our family dog rests while we work hard raising chickens. The life of a dog!

When chicks first come to our farm, they look like little balls of fuzz—with small beaks and skinny legs!

It takes us eight weeks to raise a batch of chickens. Then the chickens are taken away, and we start raising a new batch. In one year, we take care of five batches of chickens—that's 475,000 chickens!

Sometimes I can't believe how many chickens we take care of during the year. With all the chickens we raise, we feed a lot of families.

My family and I like to be together. I'm on the far right.

When my family first bought the farm, we didn't know anything about raising chickens. The man who sold the farm to us was really helpful. He spent a whole year teaching our family what to do. All seven of us learned about chickens together. At the end of the year, we were ready to run the business ourselves.

On a normal day, we get up between 5:00 and 5:30 in the morning. Then we say our morning prayers until 6:00 in the morning. After that, we start school. But we don't go to a regular classroom—Mom teaches us our school subjects at home. By going to school here, we can do our daily chores in between our studies. It's a good thing, because our farm gets pretty busy, especially when we get a batch of new **chicks**, or baby chickens.

We work just as hard on our homework as we do on our farm.

Just before the chicks arrive, we look in the chicken houses one last time.
They have to be clean for our new chicks.

We raise chickens for a **processing plant**, a place where chickens are made into food. Before we get our chicks, workers at the plant take care of them until they **hatch**, or break out of their eggs. The chicks are hatched in **incubators**.

An incubator is a machine that keeps eggs warm, so chicks will grow. The eggs stay in incubators for twenty-one days. Then the chicks hatch, and it's time for us to start raising them.

12

Once the delivery truck arrives, we start unloading the chicks and making them comfortable.

Workers from the plant deliver the chicks to us when they are four to eight hours old. The workers bring the chicks to our three chicken houses. We have two small houses and one big house. Each one has two levels. They're like big apartment buildings for chickens.

A boxful of little chicks!

Mom places the new chicks under
the warm brooders.

The chicks come in boxes that are
stacked on a truck. Each box has about
100 little chicks in it. The truck drives
along the side of each chicken house.
We take the boxes off at doorways along
the way. When we get the boxes inside,
we gently tip them under **brooders.**
Brooders are metal dome-shaped covers
about 3 feet around. Heat comes down
through a hole in the middle, so the
chicks stay warm. About 800 chicks
huddle under each brooder.

The chicks are used to high temperatures. Under the brooders, they seem to feel right at home.

After we dump the chicks, they're a little scared. They soon make lots of high-pitched peeping sounds. After a while, it gets very noisy. The chicks scurry around and run toward any noise they hear. Soon they settle down, though, peeping a little bit every now and again.

The chicks are a **straight run**, a mixture of girl and boy chicks. They are slightly bigger than a golf ball. Their bodies are covered with soft, yellow fuzz, or down. Each chick has a tiny **comb**, or fleshy red crest, on top of its head, too.

When you first look at our chicks, they all seem to look alike. But they vary in size and have unique features, just like people do. The chickens we raise are a kind called Cobbs. Most are white when full grown, but some have specks of brown or black.

When the chicks first come to our farm, we don't have to feed them right away. While a chick is in an egg, it gets food through the **yolk** (the yellow part of the egg). This food helps the chick stay healthy for twenty-four hours after it hatches. Then we start giving the chick tiny **pellets**. These pellets are a mixture of corn and soybean meal. The pellets give the chick all the nutrition it needs.

You can barely see the small combs on these Cobbs.

We don't know how many girl or boy chickens we have until later, when boy chickens' combs get bigger.

Ethan cuddles up to a few little chicks.
Soon they will grow to be chickens.

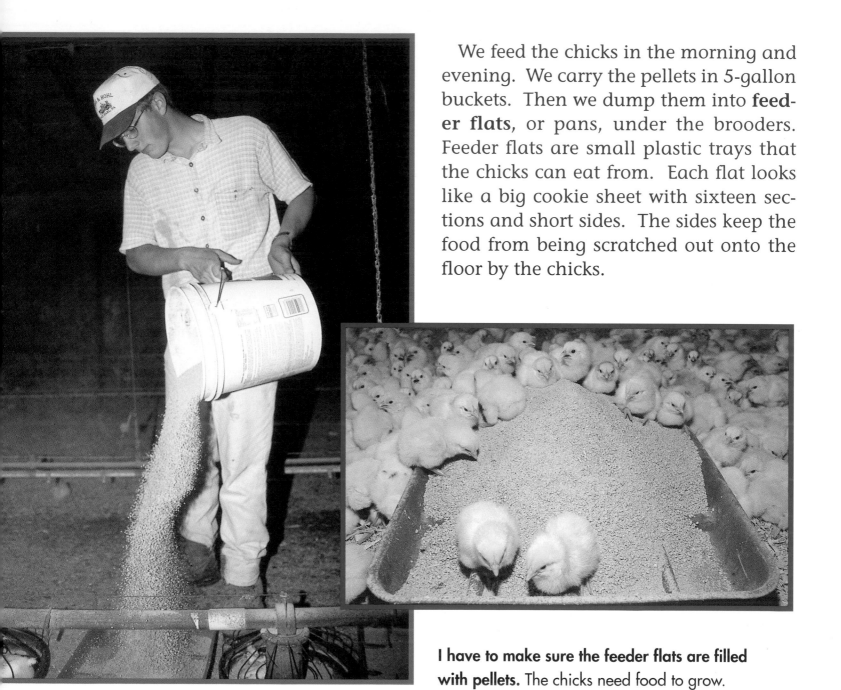

We feed the chicks in the morning and evening. We carry the pellets in 5-gallon buckets. Then we dump them into **feeder flats**, or pans, under the brooders. Feeder flats are small plastic trays that the chicks can eat from. Each flat looks like a big cookie sheet with sixteen sections and short sides. The sides keep the food from being scratched out onto the floor by the chicks.

I have to make sure the feeder flats are filled with pellets. The chicks need food to grow.

We make sure the chicks always have enough food. It's a good thing, because they can get very hungry!

After ten days, our jobs get easier. We start to give the chicks bigger pellets through an automatic feeder system. This is how it works: We store pellets in two outside feed bins. As the chicks eat, the feed bins drop the pellets into a pipeline. The pipeline takes the pellets to another bin, called a feeder. The chicks eat from this feeder. We just have to make sure the feed bins are always full.

We also give the chicks water through an automatic water system. Water runs through another pipeline. This pipeline is close to the ground, next to the brooders. It has small nipples that drip water when the chicks peck at them. The chicks can drink as much, and as often, as they want. As the chicks grow, we raise the pipeline to make sure they can reach the nipples.

This growing chicken has feathers now!

It's fun to watch the chicks get bigger. When they are about ten days old, they start to lose their yellow down. Now feathers begin to appear all over their bodies. By the time they're fourteen days old, chicks aren't yellow anymore. Their feathers may be white, black, or brown, depending on the chicken. Once they have their feathers, they're called chickens, not chicks.

Boy chickens are called roosters, and girls are called hens. We can tell them apart by their combs. Roosters usually have larger and brighter combs than hens.

20

When the chickens are fourteen days old, we give them a **vaccine**. This vaccine keeps our chickens from getting a disease that can affect their breathing. We give them the vaccine through the water system. When a chicken drinks the water, it also drinks the vaccine.

Vaccines help our chickens to keep growing strong.

Helping our chickens stay healthy is more than just feeding them, giving them water to drink, and keeping them safe from diseases. The houses they live in need care, too.

To keep our chickens healthy, we put a vaccine in the water. Chickens love water!

We do a lot to keep our chickens healthy.

More WORK to Do

Dad and I do many jobs that help keep the chicken houses healthy for our chickens. One of our jobs is to make sure the **thermostats** and fans are working properly. A thermostat helps keep temperatures the same throughout the day and night. Fans help thermostats do their jobs by removing heat from the chicken houses. Temperature is really important to a chicken's health. It needs to be just right, or our chickens could get sick.

I have to make sure the thermostat is doing its job.

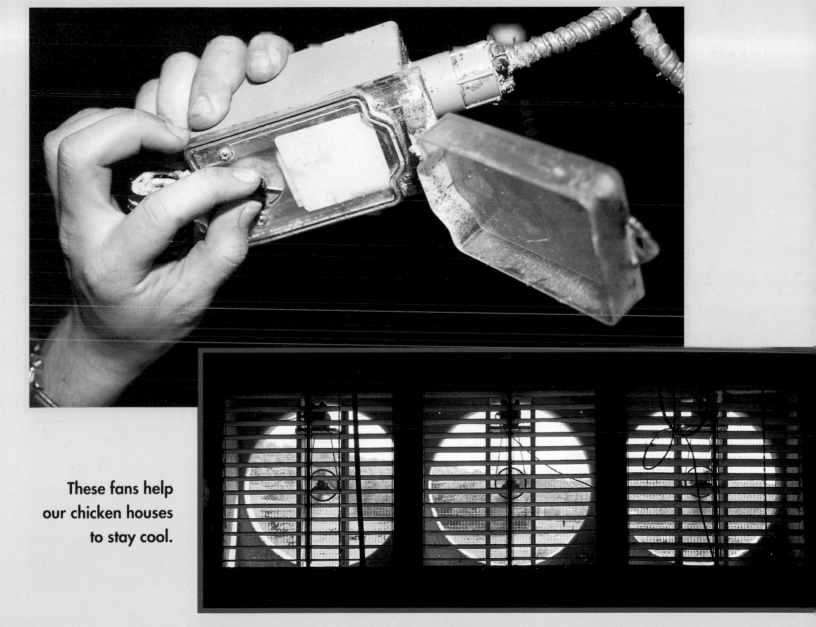

These fans help
our chicken houses
to stay cool.

Dad and I also check the **fogger system.** This system is used mostly in the summer, when it's very hot. It has a lot of nozzles that spray a mist of water into the air. The fans blow the mist and keep the temperature cool. This way, the chickens won't get too hot. The fans also keep fresh air flowing through the chicken houses. Without fresh air, the houses can get very stinky.

This nozzle sprays water that helps the chicken houses stay cool in the summer.

Jadon and Ethan took these chickens outside to explore. Chickens seem to like soft, fresh grass.

One of my weekly jobs is to flush out the water lines. I do this to get the warm water and air bubbles out. If a chicken sucks in too many air bubbles and doesn't drink enough fresh water, it could die. To flush out the water, I turn on a valve in the chicken house. The air bubbles and warm water are forced out. Then fresh water runs through the lines.

Every week, Dad checks the 400 lightbulbs in the chicken houses. He changes any that have burned out. Lights burn out once in a while, because we keep them on all day and night. We do this so the chickens believe it's always daytime. When it's daytime, chickens are more active, and they eat more. Light helps our chickens grow and grow!

Flushing out the water lines in all three houses takes me about thirty minutes.

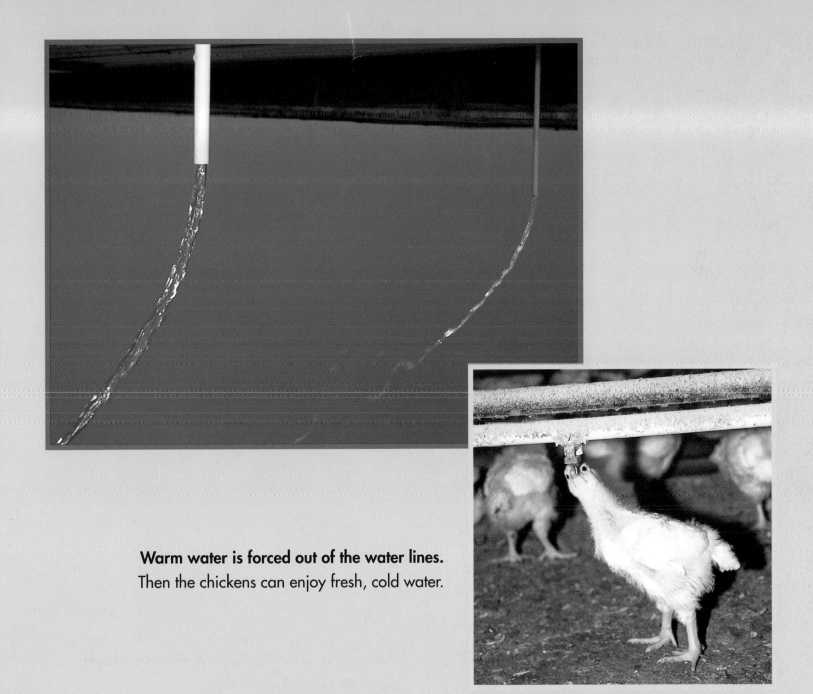

Warm water is forced out of the water lines.
Then the chickens can enjoy fresh, cold water.

Even with our best care, some chickens don't survive.
We find most of these chickens during the first four weeks.

We do our best to take care of the chickens, but not all of them survive. Some are born weak. Others get sick. Every few days, we **cull** the flock, or look for dead chickens. This is a job I don't look forward to.

When we find dead chickens, we have to pick them up and put them into a bucket. Then we carry the bucket to a covered barrel outside. Even though these chickens have died, they can still be used to make food for other animals. Every other day, a company takes the barrel of chickens away. The company uses the chickens to make pet food.

These grown chickens will soon leave our farm.

Every week a man from the processing plant comes to our farm. He makes sure we're doing everything right to raise healthy chickens. He inspects the food and water, and he checks the temperature in each house. He also examines the chickens to see if they are in good condition.

While the chickens live at our farm, we work hard to keep them fed and to make sure they stay healthy. Soon the chickens will be ready to leave.

We can't believe how fast the weeks go. It's time for our chickens to leave the farm.

Goodbye Chickens— Hello CHICKS

After we've raised our chickens for eight weeks, it's time for them to go to the processing plant. The plant sends six men, called chicken catchers, to catch every chicken.

When it's dark and quiet, the chickens rest.

Before the catching starts, we turn off the lights so the chickens think it's time to rest. While the chickens are resting, the catchers back their truck up to one end of a chicken house. At the opposite end, they open the door and put a huge fan in front of it.

The chickens cover the floor like a plush white carpet.

When the catchers go into a house, the floor is covered with chickens. It looks like a plush white-feathered carpet, with patches of brown and black. The chicken catchers start on the top level and work their way down. The lights are still off and will stay that way until the last chicken is caught!

When the catchers begin, they quickly grab chickens by one of their legs. They hold three chickens in one hand, and two in the other. The chickens don't want to be caught, so they flutter about and try to get away. (They would probably love to fly away, but chickens can't fly—their bodies are too heavy.) The fan pulls out the dust that the chickens raise when they run around.

Soon there is lots of noise and running about. The chickens try everything to get away from the catchers.

With so much going on, I don't know how these men manage to catch every chicken.

With all of the chickens squawking and the fan roaring, it's very noisy. The sound is so loud that we have to wear earplugs to protect our hearing.

I'm glad we wear earplugs. Otherwise our ears would start to hurt from the noise.

These squawking chickens are safe in their cages.

After the men catch the chickens, they put them in small cages. As the small cages become full, the men put them into a bigger one. This cage holds about 360 chickens! All the cages are stacked and strapped onto the truck. The back and sides of the truck are open, so the chickens can get air.

After the men catch all the chickens and put them in cages, the cages are loaded onto the truck.

It takes the chicken catchers about three hours to clear out an entire house. It usually takes about one and a half days to empty all three houses.

After the catchers are done, they take the chickens to the processing plant. The plant uses the chickens to make food for people.

The truck is ready to take the chickens away.

After the chickens leave, the floor is a mess!

After eight weeks of raising chickens, the chicken house floors are filthy. They are covered with food, feathers, and chicken droppings. It's time to clean up! To do this, we raise the brooders almost to the ceiling, so they are out of our way. Then we use a forklift to take a small tractor up to the second level of each house.

We've got work to do! This tractor helps me clean up the messy floors.

I shove all the waste down this hole. Then we can take it away.

We use the tractor to push the waste through many holes in the center of each building. The waste drops down to the first floor. Then we clean the first floor, scooping up all of the waste and loading it onto our truck. Dad takes the waste to a mushroom house, where it is used to help mushrooms grow.

When the houses are clean, we blow wood shavings into them. To do this, Dad first brings the shavings to the farm in a trailer. Then he puts a pipe into the trailer. When we're ready, a machine blows the shavings through the pipeline, into the chicken houses. We spread the wood shavings over the floor to make a thick bed for the next group of chicks.

It's fun to watch the floor fill up with soft wood shavings!

After we get the houses cleaned up, we have a few days before the new batch of chicks arrive. Sometimes we take a trip to a historical place, so we can learn about it. Other times, we visit family and friends, or we stay at home and enjoy the peace and quiet. Soon the trucks will bring thousands of new chicks to our farm. Then the eight-week process will start all over again.

When we have a break, Ethan likes to play. He especially likes to ride his bike.

We work hard, but we always find time to play.

My family and I like working together to take care of the chickens. It's hard to believe that we care for about half a million chickens in one year. Raising all these chickens means we're providing food for lots of families.

My mom and dad say that more chickens than people live in the world. They tell me that the number of chickens is growing faster than the number of people. If that's true, I'm thinking about having my own chicken farm someday!

I like raising chickens and living on our farm.

Fun Facts about CHICKENS

A chicken has sharp eyesight. ● *It can even see in color.*

SOME CHICKENS LOVE DUST BATHS. They roll around in the dirt to get rid of bugs that are on their skin and in their feathers.

Did you know that chickens don't have teeth? When a chicken eats, it picks up a pellet and uses its tongue to throw it back into its throat.

There are more than **50 breeds** of chickens in the world.

A CHICKEN HAS GREAT HEARING— IT CAN HEAR SOUNDS LONG BEFORE IT HATCHES FROM AN EGG!

Some hens lay 350 eggs per year.

Some chickens lay eggs that are brown—some are even greenish-blue!

THE LARGEST KIND OF CHICKEN CAN GROW TO BE 14 POUNDS.

Learn More about CHICKENS

Books

McDonald, Mary Ann. *Chickens*. Chanhassen, MN: The Child's World, Inc., 1998. This book introduces the physical features of chickens, how chickens clean themselves, and how some eggs are used for food.

Miller, Sara Swan. *Chickens*. New York: Children's Press, 2000. This colorful book has all kinds of chicken facts. Read about a chicken's life on a small farm, different breeds of chickens, and what chickens like to do.

Stone, Lynn M. *Chickens Have Chicks*. Mankato, MN: Compass Point Books, 2001. Learn about baby chickens, what they do, and how they grow up.

Websites

American Egg Board
<http://www.aeb.org>
This kid-friendly site has lots of great information about eggs. Learn about egg nutrition and find definitions to egg-related words in an egg-cyclopedia. Follow the link to Kids and Family, where you'll find ideas for decorating eggs, egg facts, and recipes made with eggs.

Feathersite
<http://www.cyborganic.com/People/feathersite/Poultry/BRKPoultryPage.html>
If you want to see pictures of chickens, this is the place! View different breeds of chickens, tiny chicks, and other kinds of poultry here. Also read about how to raise chicks.

Kids Farm
<http://www.kidsfarm.com>
Here's a site that was created by people who live on a Colorado ranch. Read about their life on the ranch and about all kinds of animals that live there. Learn about different animal sounds, farm equipment, and food that grows on the ranch. Have fun with crossword puzzles and coloring books, too.

GLOSSARY

brooders: heated dome-shaped covers that keep chicks warm

chicks: baby chickens

comb: a red crest on the top of a chicken's head. Roosters have larger combs than hens.

cull: to remove dead chickens

feeder flats: food trays that chicks eat from. The trays are divided into sixteen sections, with short sides to keep the food from being scratched out.

fogger system: a system that sprays a mist of water into the air to keep the air cool

hatch: to come out of an egg

incubators: machines that keep eggs warm so the eggs can hatch

pellets: chicken feed that is full of vitamins and other nutrients

poultry: birds that people raise for food. Chickens, geese, ducks, and turkeys are kinds of poultry.

processing plant: a place where chickens are made into food to be sold

straight run: a mixture of boy and girl chicks

thermostats: automatic devices that control temperature

vaccine: a substance given to an animal that helps its body fight off diseases

yolk: the yellow part of an egg. The yolk provides food to a chick before it hatches.

INDEX

About the AUTHOR

Judy Wolfman is a writer and professional story-teller who teaches workshops on storytelling, creativity, and writing. She also enjoys writing and acting for the theater. She has published three children's plays, numerous magazine articles, short stories, poems, finger plays, and Carolrhoda's *Life on a Farm* series. A retired schoolteacher, Ms. Wolfman has two sons, a daughter, and four granddaughters. She lives in York, Pennsylvania.

About the PHOTOGRAPHER

David Lorenz Winston is an award-winning photographer whose work has been published by *National Geographic World,* UNICEF, and the National Wildlife Federation. In addition to his work on the *Life on a Farm* series, Mr. Winston has photographed farm animals for many years. He has also taught elementary school. In his spare time, he enjoys playing the piano at his home in southeastern Pennsylvania.